Routledge Library Editions

ICONOCLASTES

SHAKESPEARE

CRITICAL STUDIES
In 36 Volumes

ICONOCLASTES

Or

The Future of Shakespeare

HUBERT GRIFFITH

Routledge
Taylor & Francis Group
LONDON AND NEW YORK

First published in 1927

Published in 2005 by Routledge
2 Park Square, Milton Park, Abingdon, Oxon, OX14 4RN
Simultaneously published in the USA and Canada by Routledge
605 Third Avenue, New York, NY 10017

*Routledge is an imprint of the Taylor & Francis Group, an
informa business*

First issued in paperback 2013

The publishers have made every effort to contact authors/copyright holders
of the works reprinted in *Routledge Library Editions – Shakespeare*. This has
not been possible in every case, however, and we would welcome
correspondence from those individuals/companies we have been unable to
trace.

These reprints are taken from original copies of each book. In many cases
the condition of these originals is not perfect. The publisher has gone to
great lengths to ensure the quality of these reprints, but wishes to point
out that certain characteristics of the original copies will, of necessity, be
apparent in reprints thereof.

British Library Cataloguing in Publication Data
A CIP catalogue record for this book
is available from the British Library

Iconoclastes

ISBN 13: 978-0-415-35291-8 (hardback)
ISBN 13: 978-0-415-84827-5 (paperback)

Miniset: Critical Studies

Series: Routledge Library Editions – Shakespeare

Pausanias having ceased, Aristodemus said that it came to the turn of Aristophanes to speak ; but it happened that, from repletion or some other cause, he had an hiccough which prevented him ; so he turned to Eryximachus, the physician, who was reclining close beside him. and said : " Eryximachus, it is but fair that you should cure my hiccough, or speak instead of me until it is over." " I will do both," said Eryximachus ; " I will speak in your turn, and you, when your hiccough has ceased, shall speak in mine. Meanwhile, if you hold your breath some time, it will subside."—*The Banquet of Plato* (Shelley's translation).

The conversation does not end quickly :
Prattling and babbling, what a lot he says !
Only when one is almost dead with fatigue
He asks at last if one isn't finding him tiring.
(One's arm is almost in half with continual
    fanning :
The sweat is pouring down one's neck in streams.)
Do not say that this is a small matter :
I consider the practice a blot on our social life.
I therefore caution all wise men
That August visitors should not be admitted.—
    Satire on Paying Calls in August: Chinese,
      3rd Century, Arthur Waley's translation).

" You prick us, do we not bleed ? "—SHYLOCK.

ICONOCLASTES

OR

The Future of Shakespeare

BY

HUBERT GRIFFITH

LONDON
KEGAN PAUL, TRENCH, TRUBNER & Co., LTD,
NEW YORK : E. P. DUTTON & Co.

To

TWO SPORTING GENTLEMEN

Sir Barry Jackson
H. K. Ayliff

*Printed in Great Britain
by Mackays Ltd., Chatham.*

ICONOCLASTES

CHAPTER I

THE UNHAPPY CLASSICS

THERE is one word which, above all others, occasions shame, dread, and embarrassment in the breasts of count-less thousands of intelligent persons who hear it. Many things in their turn have the faculty of boring the average man, be he who he may.

But there is one dislike common to an overwhelming preponderance of human-ity. It is found in a short word, a simple word, but a word that in itself sums up all the boredoms, liberates all the antagonisms, concentrates all possible ingenuities of dullness, and casts over them one pall of aching and intolerable despond. And that word is the word 'classic.'

Why should the classics in general be looked upon (except in circles vaguely scholastic) with this rancour of hatred, as in sober truth they are? It is not that 'classic' implies 'art,' and that art in general is unpopular. Art, on the contrary, is highly popular. Art, in some form or another, turns out to be just as essential as bread. If any particular man in the street does not like opera, he nevertheless has his bit of jazz on the gramophone. If he doesn't like pictures, he goes to 'the' pictures. If he doesn't read Proust, he reads the well-beloved author who for a plot recurs so frequently to the theme of a girl who dresses up as a boy and rides the favourite to victory in a horse-race.

Art is popular. And it is not even true, though it comes nearer the truth, to say that the classics of art are unpopular

[6]

merely because it needs a higher degree of trained intelligence to appreciate great art than it does to appreciate crude art. A very great deal of classic art (of Wagner, of Mozart, of Shakespeare, for example) is easy and obvious enough in its beauty to appeal to a quite brutishly innocent intelligence, provided (a) that that intelligence has not been corrupted from decent and primitive brutishness into something worse beforehand, and (b) that the work in question is adequately performed.

To come to the main argument : the word classic is detested because it is generally taken to mean ' dead ' ; because its leading exponents take every precaution to keep it dead ; and because, of the two possible meanings of the word, the second and much more important one, the one that means ' life,' has been almost entirely forgotten.

A definition of the word classic—one that would be accepted almost everywhere by classical enthusiasts—would run much as follows : ' an ancient and digni-

[7]

fied and honourable work of art, one that past generations have looked up to, and that the present admires; that still carries about it the fragrance and rarity of a departed age, a message of contact with men and with modes of life that are lost—apart from the works that they left —in the night of time.' It is a definition that covers, in its way, almost all the works of art that can be called classic, Athenian and Elizabethan drama, the marbles of Pheidias and Michelangelo, the poetry of medieval France, Molière and Cervantes, Fragonard and Marlowe, Goethe and Chekhov.

There are some people, moreover, who see in this ' distance ' of the classic its chief charm and attraction—who add archeological and historical and senti- mental value to it, until an exquisite something, born out of this ' sense of the past,' can become, to them, of definite value in itself, like the patina that settles on a bronze that has stood centuries in the open.

It can be carried—and by sensitive and

intelligent people—to lengths undreamed of by those who do not fall under this particular spell. Discussing with a very alive and ingenious critic the other day the matter of presenting a Greek play 'in masks,' I gleaned something of the following. That the play, as it had originally been done in masks, had better be done in masks now. That, as it had been done originally in a dug-out open-air theatre, it would be better if it could be done in a dug-out open-air theatre now. That, to maintain the pure integrity of its faithfulness to the original, the actors should wear boots two feet high (as they did in Attica, but which would now, all unaccustomed, prevent them from moving), and that (to destroy all individuality in their voices—their expression having gone already) they should speak through megaphones in their masks, Attic fashion.

" But what about language ? " I asked. My friend pondered a little and then said : " The original Greek." I asked him if he understood Greek well enough to allow him to follow the spoken language, and he said "No." I then asked him if he remembered that no living Englishman had really any idea of how ancient Greek was pronounced, even to the extent of making it barely intelligible to an Athenian. (Would an uneducated school-child reading Racine, and using Veenuss for Vénus, be recognized as speaking French by a Frenchman?) He replied that he was aware of this. But he still maintained that *some* of the sounds might come out right, and that this dim fidelity to the original was in itself so precious as to outweigh the advantages of the best English translation.

The gentleman of those arguments was, in all other matters, by no means lacking in shrewdness, sense of proportion, or sense of humour. Shortly afterwards, he went off and wrote a perfectly vulgar revue, and his revue had in it some of the best music-hall lyrics ever written.

I have gone into this point-of-view in some detail, for it, or a point-of-view like it, is held by many people who are among

the most ardent supporters of the classics.
Linked on to it, is the point-of-view that
venerates the classics for their ancestry
and their dignity, their proud association
with other things beside themselves.
Chaucer is the 'Father of English
Poetry' (instead of being just a good
poet), and Marlowe is the 'Morning-Star'
of Shakespeare (instead of standing on his
own legs as the author of the marvellous
Invocation to Helen). Scribe is the
inventor of the modern domestic comedy,
and led to Sardou ; and Sardou invented
the 'well-made' play, and led to Ibsen—
all very much beside the point when it
comes to considering Scribe, Sardou, and
Ibsen as entertainers, or providers of fun,
beauty, or drama.

About the Elizabethan period of our
own drama—a period of intense and
bustling activity—a huge mass of erudition has grown up. Kyd wrote *The
Spanish Tragedy*—the perfect type of
'ghost drama,' and 'revenge drama'
derived from Seneca—and also probably
wrote the earlier *Hamlet*, later to be stolen

by Shakespeare. (Therefore Seneca and Kyd are both important.) Shakespeare himself put the passage about the " imperial votaress " into *A Midsummer Night's Dream* in honour of Queen Elizabeth, and the " King's evil " speech into *Macbeth* as a compliment to King James. (Therefore the " King's evil " speech and the " imperial votaress " passage are both important, and so, too, are Queen Elizabeth and King James.) And, as certain troupes of players used to roam the country and the Continent with a mangled and mutilated and pirated version of *Hamlet*, taken down by an overdriven shorthand-writer sitting in the Globe Theatre and missing out all the best bits—therefore the Continental troupes and the shorthand-writer and the resultant ludicrous First Quarto version are all of the highest importance, and the edition is bought for great prices, and played in the London theatre of a Sunday evening, to the general boredom.

Such it is to be a classic ; and I have only drawn at random from a rag-bag of a mind certain scraps of information that must be common property to many people who, like myself, have never thought of reading the hundreds of volumes available in a library were anything like real erudition on the subject of Shakespeare sought after.

Sir Arthur Quiller-Couch has an illuminating passage in his latest book on Shakespeare. He is writing about the workmanship of *Macbeth*, about Shakespeare as a practising playwright, as a man who had an audience to entertain in a theatre. Says Sir Arthur, after denying that he will go into all the countless points of scholarship with which commentators usually deluge the play : " If, however, we spend a little time in considering *Macbeth* as a *piece of workmanship* (or artistry, if you prefer it), we shall be following a new road which seems worth a trial—better perhaps worth a trial just because it lies off the trodden way." Sir Arthur is not here being ironic. He is simply implying that poor Shakespeare is a Classic. He is implying that, writing three hundred years after his death, and possibly the three-hundredth book that has been written about him, he is actually following a " new road "—plunging recklessly into the jungle off the " trodden way "—when, if you please, he ventures to talk of Shakespeare, not as a plaster-of-Paris pterodactyl in the Crystal Palace gardens, an extinct animal, but as a practising playwright who had substantially very much the same job to do as has Mr Frederick Lonsdale. The Classics are treated three-quarters as history, and the common gorge revolts from them.

I will now, with your permission, set up an opposition point-of-view as to what constitutes a classic. It is not a new one, but it is so habitually forgotten that, re-stated, it may even take on an air of originality.

A Classic is simply a work of such intense vitality that it is always modern. This is its one test, its only test.

It owes nothing in advantage to the fact that it was made long ago. Its antiquity merely sets silly people seeing it in a wrong light.

THE FUTURE OF SHAKESPEARE

Historical associations that may have grown up round it—considerations of the works that grew out of it, or the works that it derives from—are pure irrelevancies. They encumber it, and wrap it in a pall of death, and, were such a thing possible, would put out its spark of everlasting life.

Sentimental associations degrade it. A button, a menu-card, a handkerchief, a second-rate work of art will satisfy the ' sense of period ' in anyone who has the sense developed. To use a first-rate work of art for such a purpose is to waste it. Moreover, the first-rate work of art is not even good for the purpose. Its chief point as a first-rate work of art is that it rises utterly clear of its period.

The Classic of art owes its position to one thing and to one thing only : that in the absolute quality of its achievement it is supreme and has never been surpassed. All other considerations—date, time, place, conditions of production, historical significance—have no bearing on it whatsoever.

ICONOCLASTES

The inessential trivialities of Greek drama are masks, stilts, chalk-pit theatres, groups of young ladies trained in an adequately gloomy method of intoning choruses.

Oedipus, in whose string of crudities and impossibilities no human being can ever have believed, is a true classic of the pedants, worthy for ever to be played in glaring masks and two-foot stilts, and whatever other ingenuities may bring it nearer the Mumbo-Jumbo solemnities of a South-Sea Islander. It is a bedlamite play. Its hero *has it predicted to him* that he shall murder his father and marry his mother. He thereupon goes out and slays the first old man that he sees, and pays his addresses to the only lady of forty whose identity he never bothers to discover. The *commonsense* of an imbecile would have counselled him better . . .

Oedipus is remote—a curiosity.

But when we come to *The Trojan Women* . . .

The Trojan Women was produced in London immediately after the War.

THE FUTURE OF SHAKESPEARE

There was no time or money for an elaborately Greek production—a few nondescript robes, the limited lighting resources of the Old Vic. of those days, a couple of fine actresses[1] in the two chief women's parts. But that production, played before an audience that had just come through a war of its own, and that therefore presumably knew a little what war was, was almost intolerable in the intensity of the emotion that it evoked.

Here at last was a classic that deserved the name—a play that was modern to the last twist that it could give to the lacerated nerves. Change nothing. Cut nothing —save only one word of the title : call it, not *The Trojan Women*, but *The Women*—of any clime, race, or period that has ever endured a war. Dress it in any clothes, or no clothes, or Victorian bustles and leg-of-mutton sleeves. The essentials remain utterly unchanged. A man—who happened to be an Athenian poet but who might have been a modern French journalist like M. Henri Barbusse

[1] Miss Thorndike, Miss Beatrice Wilson.

—is saying the last word on the subject of all wars, and saying it in terms that after two thousand years the most enlightened feeling of civilized humanity has not a syllable to add to. The play might have been written yesterday about yesterday. Or it might have been written in the future about the future. It will still be modern (if wars still persist) when the earth is a thousand years older.

There are also, of course, plays that fall half within the category of *Oedipus* and half within that of *The Trojan Women*— half responding to our own truest and deepest feeling, and half, like *Oedipus*, not recognizable as human, and therefore mere curiosity. Where does *Romeo and Juliet* come ? Has Romeo's long string of puns (in which he proclaims himself a witty Renaissance gentleman) any meaning to a modern audience ? What of the crudest of his badinage with Mercutio ? They have no meaning at all, for they are merely unintelligible. The actors rush through them, hoping for the best, and laughing very heartily themselves to

cover the discomfiture of the audience.
But the moonlit love-scene and the lament
in the tomb are made of the sentiments—
raised to the *nth* power of splendour and
beauty—that any young man might feel
for any young girl either now or in the
hereafter.

The point I wish to make is this : that
we play *Romeo and Juliet* only for the
things in it that appeal intimately and
poignantly to us—for that which has no
more of the sixteenth century in it than it
has of the sixth or sixtieth. We play it
for its modern (or immortal) part, the
part of it which is immortal because it is
modern. All that we don't understand
in it is just as much trash to our ears as
would be the insertion of a couple of pages
of last year's *Ally Sloper*.

The foregoing applies to all the arts
and their masterpieces in whatever
medium, in whatever manner they are
painted, sung, carved, or written.

To the historian, the Van Eycks are
important because they invented the
process of oil-painting. The painter, or

the lover of painting, doesn't trouble about this. His sole interest in the Van Eycks is that they used their new-found medium with extraordinary beauty. Velasquez has no emotional appeal for anyone as being the leader of the school of seventeenth-century Spanish painting. What matters now about Velasquez is that if any painting of his were taken and hung in a modern gallery—the child with the blonde hair who looks out with such beauty from her canvas in the Louvre— she would still make every living painter bow the knee in awe and envy.

I will now recapitulate shortly the argument of this chapter.

A classic may, by a few earnest people, be smothered under such a weight of learning and irrelevant association that the ordinary man flees—and flees rightly —from it in a dread of a tedium that he feels is not to be borne.

But the arts, in essence, are very simple things. They are the expression of an emotion.

Painting is the expression of emotion

by the beauty of paint. The materials of painting are unchangeable, and therefore painting is unchangeable. All histories of art should be torn up, for they have nothing to do with painting at all.

Music is the expression of emotion by the beauty of sound. Sounds, with the coming of orchestration, have grown more complex, but their business remains exactly the same. The orchestra of the *Götterdämmerung* may convey an intenser emotion than the song of a Sicilian shepherd. It may, or it may not. But whether it does or not is the only question that matters. Listening will tell one. But all histories of music are irrelevant, and should be torn up.

Drama is the art of arousing emotion by staging a conflict of will, character, intelligence, aspiration—whatever you like to call it. Men do not change, or change only infinitesimally slowly. The primitive passions seem to remain singularly unaltered from the earliest times of which we have any record, and the subtler aspirations are disconcertingly present in any literature we have, since literature first took shape. All histories of drama are quite beside the point. The true judgment on any drama, written at any time within the last two thousand years, is to be found by asking how it applies to oneself and to one's next-door neighbour to-day.

These considerations are of varying importance to each of the arts that I have mentioned. Painting they have no effect on. The pedants can do nothing to a picture. They can put it back in its original church (in a bad light) instead of leaving it in its gallery in a good light. But this is the extent of the damage that they can do. As regards sculpture, they can forbid the Elgin Marbles having their faces washed, holding that London grime is no doubt as good as Greek sunlight by way of forming a patina ; and in music they can suppress Wagner's re-scoring of Beethoven's *Ninth Symphony*, though Wagner clearly and obviously re-touched only where Beethoven himself would have re-touched had certain instruments of his orchestra attained, in his day, the added compass that they afterwards did in Wagner's. But this is all the interference that they can accomplish with sculpture and music.

When we come to drama, however, it is another pair of shoes. Drama needs the strenuous collaboration of other people before it can become drama at all. The pedants, *i.e.*, those who believe that a classic is a " classic " and not something essentially modern, can accomplish miracles. They can get hold of drama, and can so deal with it that alike the wise man and the foolish man, the rich man and the shilling gallery, will fly for relief to " The Pyjamas in Mabel's Room," and never go near another good play again. Shakespeare, presumably the greatest dramatist of all time, is a dramatist who, in his own city of London, has not made a sixpence for his backers in the last twenty years.

CHAPTER II

Shakespeare as Classic, and the Shakespearean Tradition

I AM now going to make two remarks that can be taken, if you like, as perverse paradoxes, but which seem to me both perfectly true, and also consistent with one another :

(*a*) Shakespeare is violently unpopular ;
(*b*) The public taste is on the whole extremely good.

(*A*) The violent unpopularity of Shakespeare may, I think, be pretty generally taken for granted.   And by unpopularity I do not mean that passers-by pause in the street to hiss his name whenever it appears on a playbill, but merely that they note it, and resolve to go to another theatre.

When Shakespeare is produced, he is

smuggled onto the stage with as much care and forethought as though he were a dangerous but talented lunatic, allowed out under surveillance to do his turn before the public. It is heralded in the Press as a feat of daring for a manager to have risked anything so fantastic. When Mr Basil Dean produced the charming pantomime *A Midsummer Night's Dream* a couple of years ago at Drury Lane— produced it at Christmas time, which was a suitable time, and with a cast that would have been the salvation of any play written—he was applauded as a man of dauntless courage and incredible artistic optimism. As Artemus Ward has it : " The Press was loud in her praises." To an unprejudiced mind, the sight of those columns of celebration and triumph over the fact that England for once was going to have a Shakespeare play at her national theatre—and a charming, easy, childish play at that, full of fun and fairies—was a revelation. The fuss could not have been greater if Mr Dean had been attempt- ing to stage some profound and philosophical work—a dramatization of the Einstein theory—or, alternately, to ram a vast tablespoonful of castor-oil down the public throat. (In point of fact, the directors of the theatre who protested against the production were perfectly in the right. The play ran ten or twelve weeks, and—with most of the artists accepting half-salary—just paid its way. A musical comedy immediately followed it, ran a year, and made a quarter-of-a-million pounds.)

Shakespeare can be made tolerable as a managerial proposition only if a star actor—and a very particularly star actor, be it understood—will appear in him, or if something extraneous and quite outside the nature of the play is brought into it. Mr John Barrymore, being the star-tragedian from the other side of the Atlantic, is allowed to have an eight-weeks go at *Hamlet* in London. He has to wait three years to get a theatre to do it; his coming is heralded with more publicity than the arrival of a new American ambassador; but ultimately he is allowed to have it. Miss Jane Cowl, having excited a vast amount of interest in herself in a long line of vampish modern parts, is allowed to make the attempt at Juliet in New York (and a very notable attempt I can believe it to have been). If the twelve most beautiful Follies girls were set to dance a ballet on the heath in *Lear*, or *Macbeth's* three witches were turned into three nymphs and winners of international beauty-competitions, these plays also would be more frequently produced.

But such things, stars and fairies, are no more than anodynes—gildings, and sometimes rich and delicate gildings, to the massive dough that is Shakespeare. Without their aid, no one would swallow it, and no manager would dare to offer it either in London or in New York. And if you say that this is in some degree true of all playwrights, I reply flatly that you are mistaken. When it is known that Mr Maugham, or Mr Lonsdale, or Mr Coward is finishing a play, every manager in London wants that play, wants it as quickly as its author can finish it, and is eager to pay him large sums in advance on its chances of success. Casting, theatre, and whatnot come later. It is the *play* that he wants. (And if you add that, of course, any new play is better than any old play, even if only by reason of its novelty, I reply that this again has not hit the mark. A play by Sir James Barrie that has already run three or four hundred nights, and whose title has become a household word, is nearly always good for a run of a further three or four hundred nights when revived.)

Compare with this the basic mistrust with which any production of Shakespeare is undertaken. The ' manager guards against him with such a concentration of stars, scenery, and Press-work as though, *sans* these, he were doomed in advance to be the flattest failure of the season.

(B) The public taste is in general very good. I do not think that this needs elaborate proof or insisting on. Instances can be given of rare and delicate plays failing, and of loud and noisy ones having success. But this is inevitable. We are not yet all archangels. The simple fact remains that in the theatrical art—an art that the public knows a good deal about—a good play is more likely to succeed than a bad one. *The Constant Nymph* was, take it all in all, probably the finest play of its year in London. Dealing seriously with problems of artistic aspiration and Bohemian conduct supposedly outside the mentality of three-quarters of the public—and which, therefore, ought to have been a bar to its success—it was still one of the most successful plays of the year. Mr Maugham has two plays produced in quick succession, one palpably a good one, the other just as obviously dull and second-rate. The bad play (both had stars in them) runs a month, the good play runs its two or three hundred nights. Mr Shaw always runs. Mr —— ——[1] always fails.

[1] To be filled in from among the names of several selected candidates.

ICONOCLASTES

As regards one important branch of the theatrical art—the art of the music-halls —the public has a taste that is cultivated, catholic, and right with an invariable rightness. The music-hall art lies even nearer to its heart than that of the stage. Result : the top-liners of a music-hall bill—the Marie Lloyds, the Will Fyffes— are sifted through a sieve of accurate and penetrating public criticism. They are top-liners for only one reason : because they are the best of their kind. And from my own experience of the music-halls, I say that that kind is genius.

I will now reconcile the two statements (that Shakespeare is unpopular, and that the public taste is on the whole shrewd, sharp, and justified) in what seems to me to be a simple and entirely adequate explanation.

The explanation, put shortly, is this :—

Shakespeare in general is done so badly that it is a standing tribute to the intensity of his genius—and to a dim semi-religious superstition on the part of a dwindling number of Englishmen that Shakespeare is in some degree an ethical stimulus—that he is ever done at all.

He is unpopular because every step is taken to make him unpopular. No other playwright in the history of drama would stand the mutilations and degradations that he is called upon to bear. No other playwright in the history of drama could be so misunderstood and mismanaged, could be undertaken alternately with such a fire of misapplied zeal, and with so gross a slackness as regards the elements of good production. No one else could be the victim of so much of the love that clouds judgment, and of so much of the stupidity that makes the angels weep. I blame no individual person for this, but only the tradition. The tradition is paramount. A good producer is one who, *in one single point*, dares to break through the tradition. An ordinary, admired, and respected producer is one who will carry through the tradition to its uttermost absurdity.

ICONOCLASTES

The Shakespearean Tradition

Accompany me, please, to any Shakespearean production that you care to suggest, a comedy, a history, a drama, a romance. But I will first ask you to imagine for a moment that the play is not —oh, *not*—by Shakespeare, but is by a nameless and unknown dramatist—a poor devil who is only trying to do, as well as he is able, what all dramatists must have tried to do since the days when playwrighting began. Imagine him a man— any contemporary dramatist, if you like— trying to devise an entertainment for an audience, and doing it by the only means in his power—by making us believe that a set of real things is happening to a set of real people. For this is the end and aim of all drama. For Shakespeare, you may substitute Mr Frederick Londsale. And you can do this the more readily, for you can remember that in the course of a few centuries men do not change at all. I have put at the beginning of this book three quotations : one is the lament of a Chinese gentleman (200 A.D.) that callers are coming to tea on a hot afternoon and that they will bore him ; the second is from the discussion of Athenian philosophers, one of them being afflicted with an attack of hiccoughs, as to which of them shall make the first after-dinner speech ; the third is from the Bard himself, making his worst villain explain that he is only human like anyone else. The three quotations, spread over two thousand years, are interchangeable as regards date—or, similarly, every one of them might have been taken from yesterday's newspaper. Men do not change.

The crimes committed against commonsense, the sheer absurdities that you are now about to see—with your new outlook, remembering that the play is ' not by Shakespeare ' but is by any contemporary, dramatist—are going to begin with the rise of the curtain, and are not going to end until the curtain fall.

For your convenience, I will put some

of the minor ones under headings. They go down as :

Beards	Cutting (and Pace)
Gesture	Not-Cutting
Voices	Clowning
Laughter	

and possibly a dozen others, the aim of all of which alike is, not to make the play seem like the happenings of real things to real people, but to make the whole display as unreal, remote, ugly, and tedious as the ingenuity of man can render it.

Beards: It is difficult on the stage to speak in a beard. It is difficult on the stage to make a beard look like a beard. Nearly all beards you are going to see in the play are going to absorb at least half the author's words spoken through them, and are going to give the actor an inept, elephantine suggestion of private theatricals in addition. Beards should be abolished. If it could be proved that in Shakespeare's time all old men wore long beards, and all young men wore short

[34]

beards and moustachios, I would still say that beards should be abolished. Their effect is to give the actors themselves the impression that they are appearing in something remote and fantastic and inhuman. And actors can be remote and fantastic and inhuman enough for many other reasons without this additional handicap.

Gesture: The gesture that you will see will quickly—if you remember that Shakespeare did not write the play, but that it was written by another author—appear to you quite incredible. Men and women in their unaccustomed clothes will not be able to move, speak, sit down, enter the stage, leave the stage, greet a companion, without giving an imitation —not of how they believe people once did it, but of how no person can ever conceivably have done it. Note how the same mysterious and uncomprehended tradition seems to rule over the smallest actions. Watch two young men move off-stage at any insignificant moment of the play, say, when the principals have just finished a

[35]

scene. They will laugh, they will slap each
other on the back—many times; they
will put their arms round one another's
shoulders, and will walk into the wings,
laughing again, Ha, ha, ha. Then imagine
a producer of a modern play calling the
two young men back after a similar scene
at rehearsal. " Why do you slap each
other on the back ?   Is there anything in
the play about your having just borrowed
a fiver from a foolish acquaintance ? Who
made a joke, that you laugh ?   Do you
usually walk out into Piccadilly embrac-
ing other young men round the neck ?
In short, my good sirs, are you tight ? "
What is the answer ?   " Dear boy, we are
in Shakespeare."

Voices : There used to be an actor in
Shakespeare who played every part of a
man over forty in a high falsetto voice
that was like the scraping of slate-pencils
on a slate.   He could keep it up for an
entire evening like that.   His voice did
not wear out.   It was better at the end
of two years of such evenings than at the
beginning.   But the anguish of listening

to it had often driven me from the theatre. He was obsessed with the idea that any man over forty in Shakespeare must automatically have a falsetto voice. I used sometimes to have happy (never realized) visions of him applying for a part in a modern comedy, of his getting it, and going down to rehearsal to play the part of a modern gentleman over forty, with the slate-pencil voice all complete. And I used, in imagination, to see the producer's face of awe and amazement during his first ten seconds of utterance, and—ten seconds later again—my actor flying through the stage-door into the street as though shot up through a star-trap, with awe and amazement on *his* face this time ; and of the company settling back to its rehearsal with the mystery all cleared up and explained : " Ah, he comes from Shakespeare."

Laughter : See above, *Gesture.* It is a commonplace in everyday life that a man who laughs at nothing is an imbecile. Either because the producer tells them to, or because the producer is slack and doesn't tell them not to, half the characters in any Shakespearean play will be endeavouring to prove themselves imbeciles. It is felt that a Shakespearean comedy must be accompanied by laughter. If the audience will not supply it, the actors will. The traditional entrance is on a laugh. The traditional exit is on a laugh. It is, in its way, the most curious part of the whole tradition. The cumulative effect of such mirth at the end of the evening will be lugubrious enough to make you drown the carpet in your tears. In a modern comedy such stupidity would no more be tolerated than actors who came on at each of their entrances with blacked faces and a buck-dance.

Cutting, and *Pace:* The cutting of Shakespeare is notorious, and so shall not be dealt with at any length here. Cutting is inevitable, because it is felt that, great as he is as a dramatist, we really cannot stand more than about three hours of him. Well and good. But the cutting should be done intelligently, and, when the play is a good play, it should be played with an eye to keeping in as much of the best of it as can possibly be managed in the agreed time. *Hamlet* is held to be a very good play, and is more ruthlessly cut than all the others. This is partly because it happens to be longer than all the others. But this does not account for the way it was given in London the other day. Mr Barrymore cut it as ruthlessly as it has ever been cut—in order to play the rest of it more slowly than it has ever been played ! In other words, Shakespeare having in this play arrived at his very most expressive and beautiful mastery of language, Mr Barrymore said to him : " I will take out half your words, and substitute my own personality—the beauty and expressiveness with which I move, sit, walk across the stage in silence, etc.—for the gaps I make in your text." Can one conceive Mr Shaw's emotions if an actor proposed to him to cut most of the talk out of the part of John Tanner, and to make the omissions expressive by a display of silent ' acting ' of his own ?

[39]

Not-Cutting: This is a far worse offence in its way than cutting. There is, from practical considerations—from the fact that a modern audience will not stay for four hours in a theatre—a fair justification for cutting. There is no justification at all for keeping in much that is habitually kept in, in Shakespeare. The pedants cannot have it both ways. There is everything to prove that in the printed plays as they have come down to us there is matter ' lifted ' from other writers who were not Shakespeare, worked over hurriedly, ill-assimilated, or not worked over at all. There is also every material proof that Shakespeare, turning out thirty-six plays in a short working life, managing a theatre, acting, and enjoying himself—in other words, being an extraordinarily prolific and busy man—was not always at his best in what he actually wrote. The plays vary in quality, from the best of the great tragedies, where almost every line is a masterpiece, to the less authentic of the Histories, that contain page after page of childish doggerel. No pedant or hero-worshipper can pretend that every line as we have it is immortal. In regard to the frankly feeble passages, they can save the Bard's face in either of two easy ways : by saying that somebody else wrote them, or that he wrote them himself in a hurry. But in either case the absurd outcry for doing Shakespeare ' in full ' must stop. Wherever a passage is (*a*) bad, (*b*) unintelligible to a modern audience, it should be cut without compunction.

What is an actress to do with such nonsense as :

> Till thou give joy, until thou bidst me joy
> By pardoning Mowbray, my beloved boy . . .

or an actor with the Romeo-Mercutio quips :

MER.: Follow me this jest now, till thou hast worn out thy pump; that, when the single sole of it is worn, the jest may remain, after the wearing, solely singular.

ROM.: O single-soled jest, solely singular for the singleness !

(After which Mercutio can find it in his heart to remark: " Now art thou sociable, now art thou Romeo " . . .)

It is pedantry and Bardolatry to keep them in. As regards the historical passages that I mentioned in an earlier chapter, commonsense alone should decide. The " Imperial votaress " passage happens to be turned into an entrancingly lovely lyrical outburst. Of course it should stay. The " King's evil " speech in *Macbeth* is apropos nothing in the story, comes at the worst moment of the drama to hold up the action and mystify everybody, and, of course, should go.

Clowning: Of the clowning that you are likely to see in many well-accredited Shakespearean productions, I will not trust myself to speak. It would be out of place in a provincial pantomime, and the curtain would be rung down upon it in a provincial music-hall. Poor Shakespeare's back, because he is an immortal, is supposed to be broad enough to bear it all.

I have gone into some of the minor matters—each of them remediable by a single stroke of decent care and honest attention—that make Shakespeare so perplexing and defeating to anyone who comes to him fresh with an unprejudiced mind after the best of modern acting.

(They are also, incidentally, the things that make a Shakespearean company the worst possible training-ground now-a-days for any young talent. A young actor or actress entering a Shakespearean company will become set in a way of speaking, walking, declaiming, that will render him or her unfit to take part in any modern performance until all that has been learnt has been unlearnt again. And the unlearning is no easy matter. It is a fact worth drawing attention to, that of the half-dozen finest young actors and actresses of the day—people who have made deserved reputations for themselves in the highest and hardest sorts of modern drama—not one of them has had a regular Shakespearean grounding, and two or three of them at least have hardly spoken a line of Shakespeare at all. A couple of generations ago, when all plays were still either melodramas or farces, a Shakespearean training was, of course, indispensable.)

I have not yet mentioned the major matter, to which all the other details lead up and contribute. It is this : That the huge mass of producers, actors, critics, and audiences simply do not realize (because Shakespeare is a ' classic,' and because all these things happen) that his plays are like all other plays—a sequence of as real things as possible, happening to a set of people as real as possible—to be played out to the least ounce of imaginative verisimilitude, as is any play accepted from a novice by a Sunday play-producing Society.

I have seen *Romeo and Juliet* with Romeo's part cut down to the bare cues and responses, because Juliet was a fashionable actress and Romeo was not a fashionable actor. I have seen the Council Chamber scene in *Othello*—from the very texture of the play a hurried midnight war-scene, with a Cabinet meeting going forward, and dispatches arriving, and the Commander-in-Chief suddenly called in to explain his conduct with a girl—I have seen all this rush of disturbance and emotion produced by a famous producer with such utter disregard of immediate drama as to make it a leisurely pageant-of-state scene, with the Doge on his throne in full fig, and everybody as composed and dignified as though sitting for his portrait to Bellini. I have seen the hackneyed trial-scene in *The Merchant of Venice*—not once, but every time I have seen it—produced so badly that at the dramatic climax of the thing, when Portia suddenly brings off her *coup* that is to save Antonio's life and turn the tables on Shylock—not a soul in Court, not Antonio, nor his friends, nor one of the spectators even, so much as moved a muscle of his face or body in surprise, or relief, or jubilation. Everyone in a twentieth-century audience knows the story of Portia's *coup* since his nursery. Granted. But not a producer I have ever met has brought it home to his actors that *they* are not supposed to know the end of Portia's defence before she had made a beginning. In other words, that to contemporaries in Court that day the winning stroke was a brilliant surprise, and not a foregone conclusion . . .

[45]

I have said that Shakespeare is badly produced. It is my experience that a great many modern plays are well produced. And I ask myself this : Why, if the most trivial comedy that Mr Frederick Lonsdale writes is produced with all the care accredited to genius, with its climaxes worked up, its wit intensified, its drama eked out with all the arts of suspense and surprise and subtle underlining—if all this care and forethought and brilliance is accorded to Mr Lonsdale to help him to tell a new story—why in the name of humanity and reason should people pay to see Shakespeare, who tells them an old story, and on whose head all the stupidities of three centuries are come ?

The answer, of course, is twofold. The best of Shakespeare is almost indestructible ; and there is still a section of the populace to whom Shakespeare, even at his worst, is a sort of moral emblem, something that, however dull or painful, must be endured by themselves, and to whom their children must be taken, as to Church and the dentist. I would point out that this last part of the answer by no means holds good of the future. The generation of people is fast decreasing who tolerate what bores them, for the good of their souls.

CHAPTER III

Shakespeare as Modern

I CAN no longer conceal the main purpose for which I have been blackening with ink these pleasant sheets of paper. It is to state, with the utmost possible emphasis, the belief of one critic : That the future of Shakespeare lies in doing Shakespeare as a modern playwright, either now or a thousand years hence in the time to come ; that the finest effort ever made on behalf of Shakespeare in the modern theatre was made when Sir Barry Jackson and Mr H. K. Ayliff produced a 'modern dress' *Hamlet* in London in October, 1925 ; and that Shakespeare's hold over the future, if he is to hold the future at all, will be through a Danish prince in a dinner-jacket, an Ophelia drowning herself in a short frock, and a Desdemona who

[48]

comes into the Council Chamber in an evening cloak as a girl summoned away through the night in a taxicab from a ball. Corresponding changes will have to be made when dinner-jackets, short frocks, and taxicabs are no longer modern, be it well understood.

The effect that the modern *Hamlet* made in London was profound. And by this I do not mean that it was acclaimed with triumph and ran a thousand nights, but that certain results almost as significant arose out of it. In the first place, the Press did not damn it. Two or three great papers were enthusiastic. Half-a-dozen more were guardedly favourable. The rest were guardedly unfavourable or antagonistic. But to have planned so extraordinary an outrage on an ancient British institution, the classic of classics, and to have half the daily Press seriously considering the result on its merits (and not one paper of them all shouting that Sir Barry was in the pay of Moscow) meant that the impression had gone deep. Also, that British criticism was as intelligently receptive as is to be found anywhere in the world.

In the second place, owing to the *réclame*, a certain number of people went to see a Shakespeare play who had never been to see a Shakespeare play before. In the third place, quite a large number of people actually *understood* a Shakespeare play from beginning to end who had never believed that such a thing was possible or even desirable before. And in the fourth place, a number of intelligent people were reassured. An unspoken doubt was at last set at rest. The doubt may be expressed as this : " The Swan is great as a poet. We know this. Proof : the best passage from any authentic play, from *Love's Labour's. Lost*, to the last scenes of *The Tempest.* But as a playwright ? Are we anything like so sure, in our heart of hearts, of *that ?* Think of all the fire of new blood that has come into the theatre even in the last fifty years, Shaw and Ibsen and Chekhov and the rest—how does Shakespeare as a playwright come off when compared with these ?   He is hardly an original thinker, seeing that all his finest utterances are a sublimation of the commonplace.   He had not a belief in anything in the world, holding that life itself is merely a stepping-stone to the bonfire or the ash-pit, or at best is finished off with a sleep.   Could he, again, with his Macbeths and Iagos, hold up a lamp to the quiet heart of everyday people like that of the magician Chekhov ?   Surely, in our heart of hearts, we do not compare him as a playwright *exactly* as we compare these people as playwrights with one another. After all, the weight of three hundred years must be expected to lie a little heavy upon him . . ."   No doubt a good many earnest Shakespeareans had something of this at the back of their minds.

The Kingsway production of *Hamlet* shattered these flattering illusions of modernity once and for all.   In the field of science a man's work may be exceeded or forgotten.   A first-year student now-a-days knows as much as Faraday knew at the end of his lifetime.   But in the arts a great man remains always great. The effect of *Hamlet*, played for the first time so that it *should* actually compare with the best modern playwrighting, was a rout of the moderns. *Hamlet*, in the intensity of its excitement, the freshness of its wit, the sheer immortal vitality and perversity and waywardness of all its countless characters, stood forth as the sort of play on which all the best brains of modern literature (blended into pure genius) might have collaborated—or which any one of them might have written if, in addition to his own specialized knowledge, he had been endowed with a sort of omniscient and universal humanity. Here at last one might be forgiven the rather absurd feeling : " Here is the best play in the world." Here at last one might feel, with more justification : " Here is the play that contains the germ of all other plays." And for one critic at least, after some years of theatre-going, it has remained incomparably his greatest experience in the theatre.

(As is usual in all such cases where high

novelty is offered to the public, those who abused it most loudly were those who, as they expressed it, had " studied the question carefully," but who had not somehow " actually been to the Kingsway to see it . . . " Which is a parallel to the case of any critic who writes a notice condemning a play and receives forty letters of protest through the post next morning, thirty of them beginning : " Of course, we have not actually *seen* the play in question, but . . . " A case that happens to us all.)

The extreme and overpowering beauty of the Kingsway *Hamlet* was, of course, the result of many causes. I will go through them as shortly as maybe. In the first place—though not by any means the chief place—there was the absence of all the normal *clichés* of the trade—the things that, once one has become conscious of their absurdity, turn the ordinary Shakespearean production into a travesty and an affront. Old men did not mumble through beards, or squeak in high falsetto voices. The laughter was confined exclusively to the audience.

There was no lounging and attitudinizing
and back-slapping. The play was played
at the normal pace of modern comedy,
with pauses and hesitations only at those
places where one could have said to the
actor : " Why are you hesitating ? Why
are you making that pause ? " and he
could have given the reasoned answer :
" I paused at such and such a place to
let the last sentence sink in. I hesitated
in front of that word because it is a word
which needs to be important when it
comes "—no futile general answer : " I
played the whole scene slowly because I
hoped that that would make it im-
pressive."

These details alone, the direct result of
playing the play in modern clothes and
with a company of actors who had no
link with the Shakespearean tradition,
would have made the play a light among
the darkness, a relief, a beatitude. And
if you doubt that mere change of costume
can have a profound effect upon an actor's
technique, I reply : " An actor is chained
to his clothes. A man in ordinary life

moves and holds himself slightly differently in every different dress he wears—in evening dress, when booted for riding, in flannels.   Before an actor can comport himself in the extreme unfamiliarity of trunk-hose, doublet, sword, and cloak—before he can avoid tripping over the sword and strangling himself with the cloak—he must have had a special series of lessons in their management.   And each of these lessons has taken him—in the direction of the pictorial, the sculpturesque, the plastic, call it what you will—a step further away from vivid life as he knows it—a step further away from the life of Oxford Street, and a step nearer to the Albert Memorial."

More, again, than what modern dress could do in the way of not hampering the illusion, it could do in the way of actually creating and sustaining the illusion.   We understand little about the details of Elizabethan clothes, still less about ancient   Danish.   The   designers   of theatrical costumes—most of them—understand not much more.   How can

they show us when the characters are in
their evening or party clothes, as they
must obviously be for some scenes, or in
their day clothes for others? Neither
we nor they know the difference. How
show that Laertes is a carefully-dressed
young man, and Osric a dandy, and how
differentiate between the social status of
the members of the King's entourage and
the party of touring actors thrown
suddenly into their midst? It cannot be
done. All such distinctions are lost to
modern eyes. A vague picturesqueness,
known generally as ' Shakespearean costume,' covers them all, and for all purposes
of marking character and rank each might
just as well be dressed in a diving-suit.
In the one case where differentiation is
attempted, in the case of poor Hamlet
himself, the attempt is disastrous. An
inky cloak has become his distinguishing
sign ; and an unchangingly inky cloak
he accordingly wears (as Mr George Robey
sticks to his bowler-hat and clerical
collar) through battles, floods, and sieges,
through flights to England, fencing-

matches and descents into Ophelia's grave, precisely as though he were a tramp without another suit of clothes to his name, or the action of the play were all over in twenty-four hours. It is, of course, spread over several months. (Here, again, no modern producer would go to such lengths to negative its logic, and make it confusing and impossible for an audience to understand.)

The producer of *Hamlet* in modern clothes can set all these things to rights with a single stroke of care expended on each of them. He can make Laertes fashionably dressed (as in the text), and he can make Osric over-fashionably dressed (as in the text). He can get a legitimate stroke of comedy out of the appearance of the touring-company at Court, their gloves a little too bright and their plus-fours a little too baggy, as is the habit of touring companies all the world over ; and he can isolate the Prince in his dinner-jacket among the courtiers who wear white ties and tails, as effectively as ever was done by the inky cloak. He can do all these things in such a way that the least point is picked up by a modern audience. And if anyone should be inclined to dismiss these points as minor points and unimportant points, may one remind him that when Sir Gerald du Maurier produces a play like *Interference*, he does *not* so arrange things that an out-of-work clerk wears identically the same style of dress as the rich employer to whom he is applying for a job ; a Harley-street specialist does *not* wear the same coat both for working in and going a journey to a distant country and for dining with a duchess ; bells do *not* ring on one side of the stage when someone is about to enter from the other ; and the parlour-maid who announces that the carriage is waiting to a drawing-room in Mayfair has a difference of speech from the girl who washes up the things in a farm-house kitchen. All of which is merely to say that Sir Gerald has no belief that any play whatever is the better for being done carelessly, and no belief but that all plays may be improved if the

producer sets out to help as intelligently
as he can the effect asked for by the
dramatist.

They are small things, but Shakespeare
thought about them, and they are as much
part of the drama as anything else that
the producer has to decide. They help
us, weak mortals that we are, to see the
characters not as the sticks and stones of
a worn-out convention, but as living,
breathing realities—a particular young
man who thinks he sees a ghost, an older
man who has once poisoned his brother
for the love of a woman, exactly as in last
week's police reports. This last aspect
of the matter is of high importance.
Shakespeare was never an ' expressionist '
dramatist, dealing in abstractions. He
worked entirely through flesh and blood.
He will go out of his way to invent a
whole scene only to show us some particular trait of Hamlet's personal character—
his moment of misgiving before the duel,
his reference to his months of practice at
fencing, his human boredom at Polonius,
his enjoyment of Osric and the grave-

digger. It is the most purely personal portrait ever drawn—being by the same hand that created Pistol and Bardolph and Falstaff for nothing but his intense love of the variety and inexhaustible idiosyncrasy of human character. If a dress-tie helps us to realize Hamlet as a young man, by all means let us have it. The divine rhetoric will look after itself none the worse for it.

This is what modern clothes can help to do, from the point-of-view of the spectators.

What they can do from the point-of-view of the actors is past telling ; and past believing by anyone who did not see the Kingsway production. I take it that the King's part is universally accepted as a bad one, and that the Queen's part is usually supposed to be worse ; that Polonius is known to be at times tedious and at other times amusing ; and that the rest of the male members of the cast, Horatio and Laertes down to poor Rosencrantz and Guildenstern, are resigned to being merely polite accessories

to help on the action—dim ghosts of an
undefeatable dullness who form a back-
ground while the principal boy of the
entertainment, the Hamlet, mouthes and
rants his speeches. Do not misunder-
stand me. I do not blame them. I know
that the principal boy often enough
insisted upon it . . .

But at the Kingsway . . . Perhaps of
all the impressions that those who saw the
production carried away, the most vivid is
the sudden realization that Hamlet is not
the principal figure in his own play.
When *all* the characters were played
properly for the first time, the very genius
of Shakespeare was seen to have defeated
itself. He had started out to write a play
with a hero, Hamlet. But he hadn't been
able to do it. Being at the very height of
his creative faculty at the time, the figures
he had put round him, the King, the
Queen, the courtiers, the servants, the
comedians, had each been drawn with such
force and perfection that each, during his
term of speech, became the principal figure
of the play, and there was therefore no

principal figure at all. Claudius, Gertrude, the shrewd, asinine, worldly-wise Polonius, Laertes, and even Horatio himself—each and all became suddenly endowed with a gigantic and appalling measure of life, straining at each other, cutting across each other's purpose, driving forward with their own hopes and ambitions and desires, until the play became, not a play about one person nor a play about six of them, but a play about twenty people, each as vitally interesting as the other, and Hamlet was left with as much importance as any other *jeune-premier* in his own history, and no more. His part merely remained the finest *jeune-premier* part ever written . . .

This collective series of miracles, I may mention, was not brought about by any collection of star-actors. Good actors there were in the cast, but few who would yet call themselves celebrities. Ophelia was a girl of nineteen making her first London appearance. All, almost by special request on the producer's part, were strangers to Shakespeare. The

THE FUTURE OF SHAKESPEARE

Hamlet, Mr Colin Keith-Johnston, was a young actor who had done some things for Mr Shaw in Birmingham and in London. He will always, by reason of his youth, by his fitting into place so admirably in the great drama, by reason of the earnest, worried, entirely convincing way in which the great lines came from him—not declaimed, but as though torn in undertones out of his heart—be my most memorable Hamlet. But he did it without for a moment laying himself out to be the 'great actor' playing the play.

To sum up the advantages that seemed to me to come out of this way of doing Shakespeare 'in modern clothes'—which was a detail, and 'as a modern play'—which was all-important. At a stroke it swept away a thousand abuses of the old tradition, just as Wagner's renovation of the operatic idea gave a new and unforeseen life to all opera. Wagner's own details were important to him in producing *The Ring*. But their reaction was much wider than this. His simple demand that *all* parts should be done as well as they

[63]

could possibly be done was something new in the era in which he launched it. And its reverberations shortly extended over the whole operatic world.

Mr Ayliff's idea lent a new and unheard-of interest to parts that had always been regarded before as the merest hackwork. It made the Queen (as she must obviously have been) a comparatively young and attractive woman—a Mrs Tanqueray rather than a Mrs Alving. It made the King into a gentleman—a great innovation this. It transformed Polonius from a clown who would have run the State of Denmark onto the rocks in twenty-four hours into an elderly politician, hit off to the life with marvellous exactitude. And —and here is the true miracle—so far from having to strain Shakespeare's lines to make them bear these interpretations, the play has never seemed to play so easily before, the producer had never found all the indications for each character so clearly on the surface of the text, never has he had so little to do in the way of ' production ' except insist that each actor should play unaffectedly to the line as the author wrote it. The play was played out in this fashion to the last thrill of its dramatic content, and when, over the dead body of Hamlet in modern fencing-clothes, the closing lines were spoken :

Fort.: Where is this sight ?
Hor.:   What is it you would see ?
If ought of woe or wonder, cease your search.

a feeling came over the theatre that a great wheel had been worthily brought full-circle, that a great epic was flawlessly ended.

Also another feeling, for most of those that saw it : that the old *Hamlet*—a *Hamlet* played any less strenuously and rigorously than this—would never hold their attention again. The keystone of the arch had been found. It was a play that truly, and not only in the lip-service of those who are afraid to practise what they preach, had stepped out of the boundaries of its own time, and could be set down in the twentieth century without a syllable of all its thousands of words needing to be altered or suppressed. The

E

Sphinx had yielded up its secret to the first touch of commonsense shed upon the subject for a hundred years.

There are two chief arguments against such a presentation of a classic—advanced always, be it understood, by those who did not take the trouble to go and see the experiment.   Those who did need no answer.

They are :

(*a*) Wasn't any part of it necessarily ' comic,' ' facetious ' ?

(*b*) How could blank verse possibly go with modern clothes ?

There is a reasonable answer to both objections.   As produced by Mr Ayliff, there was no hint of facetiousness from end to end of the play.   Mr Ayliff never ' played for laughs,' and he never got laughs, outside the atmosphere of high and subtle comedy in which Shakespeare himself bathes the play.   I am no advocate of playing the play badly in modern clothes, carelessly, facetiously, or with any less degree of intelligent atten-

tion than Mr Ayliff gave it. He had
simply chosen a method of doing it that
forces up the standard to a plane where
carelessness or ineptitude must not exist.
(As an example of good taste, there was
the room in which all the Court scenes
were played, which was in itself a beautiful
room, with a high and simple dignity in
its design.

There were the clothes, which, as
befitting people of rank, were good clothes.
The actors had also been instructed to
display that care of good manners that
differentiates a Court from a canteen.
And lastly, as intrinsic beauty is always
a thing worth having in a production when
there is no reason to the contrary, it may
be remarked that beautiful effects of line,
colour, and grouping are far more likely
to be achieved by a producer handling
modern dress than by one handling fancy
dress. Modern dress, in the mass, is more
beautiful than any reconstruction we can
make of the old dress. Up to the
eighteenth century men had the bad taste
to wear brilliant colours as well as the

women. In any modern panorama, say, a ballroom, brilliance of colour in the lights and the women's dresses will always be blended into harmony by the modern preference of plain wall surfaces—and the plain black-and-white that the men are wearing. Take away this advantage from a designer, set him to harmonize a group in which *all* the participants are wearing gaudy colours, and there are not more than two or three men in the world (outside those working for the Russian Ballet) who can evolve anything better than, as Disraeli said of Peel's policy, a " humdrum hocus-pocus.")

The misunderstanding in the matter of the blank verse and the general high-flown language in the mouths of modern-dressed actors is a more intelligent one, but can also be disposed of.

Without going into great detail, it may be taken that there are two distinct ideas of writing dialogue for the stage which have both proved themselves good and suitable ones. There is naturalistic dialogue—as, say, Mr Ervine has written

[68]

in *Jane Clegg*. And there is dialogue that is frankly unnaturalistic, a form that Mr Shaw has chosen for all his plays. In *Jane Clegg* Mr Ervine has not been flatly realistic, for he has missed out all the hesitations and repetitions that he would have had to put in if he wanted his dialogue to be photographically exact to life. But he has achieved the general effect of faithfulness that he wanted. His characters express their emotions, in general, only in such words and phrases as they would normally use in their own stations in life. When well done, it is an admirable way of writing plays. Mr Shaw's method is different. The long speeches that he gives his characters are made of the clearest, most balanced, and most trenchant prose that is now being written, the work of a master of the English language writing at leisure—and not at all the sort of thing that an ordinary man is capable of giving out in a drawing-room in real life, or that Mr Shaw himself is capable of using when he speaks extempore from a platform. This again is another admirable way of writing plays. It is an old-established convention, and a good convention, that characters in plays are always allowed to speak *better* than they would ever do in ordinary life —they are allowed, for purposes of drama, a freedom, an exactness, and a beauty that, in ordinary life, would be as much beyond them as speaking in villanelles or sonnets. And the convention is so convenient a one from all points-of-view that we notice no strain about it. We only notice a strain about it when it is badly done—*i.e.*, when the characters speak *worse* than in life. The other day there was heard in a London theatre the magnificent sentence : " You can't torture hearts and consciences, bodies and souls—*and get away with it !* "—a monument of how the semi-literary can entangle itself with the semi-colloquial, to the production of utter bathos.

Shakespeare, of course, wrote almost entirely in the convention of those who make stage dialogue a heightened and harmonized, and therefore unnaturalistic,

form of speech. He occasionally aban-
doned it—" Hoo ! say 'a. Where's ma
hat," and so forth ; but in general his
idea was to strain the language to its
limit to draw its last splendours of rhetoric
out of it. We get characters doing perfectly normal things, but explaining why
they do them in a flow of immortal
loveliness. Approve of it or not, as you
like, but do not make the mistake of
thinking that it was a convention that
died with Shakespeare, or that Elizabethan dress had anything to do with it.
Cleopatra's great closing song of

> Give me my robe, put on my crown, I have
> Immortal longings in me . . .

is only as unnaturalistic as Mr Shaw's
painter dying in a modern studio with his :
" I believe in Michelangelo, Velasquez,
and Rembrandt ; in the might of design, the mystery of colour, the message
of art that has made these hands
blessed." It is only as unnaturalistic,
and no more so. And the whole point
of it is that, spoken on the stage,

neither seems to us unnaturalistic at all.
It would need a malcontent to complain
that either were " too well written."
When Hamlet and the Court of Elsinore
are going at it in their best form, either in
modern dress or in any other dress, one's
only emotion is one of pure envy. An old
lady standing next to Turner when he
was out painting complained to him :
" Mr Turner, I don't see any such colours
in nature." " Ma'am," replied Mr
Turner, " don't you wish you could ! "
No dialogue could be too good for the
stage. When dialogue becomes maud-
lin, sententious, and wordy without
being expressive—then it is time to
complain.

I have talked at unconscionable length
on the one Kingsway production of
Hamlet because it was by far the complet-
est and most thought-out attempt that
has yet been made to do Shakespeare on
these lines. It succeeded, it seemed to
me, going to it for the first time with an
open and none too hopeful mind, beyond
any possible expectation.

THE FUTURE OF SHAKESPEARE

Two other experiments have been made : *All's Well That Ends Well,* done by Sir Harry Jackson's company, and *Othello,* done by a company of amateurs (the King's College Amateur Dramatic Society) in London. *All's Well* was only a partial success. The play itself is among the duller flights of the Bard's fancy, and although one or two scenes gained a definite sparkle of excitement when lines written three hundred years ago came pat and applicable from the lips of youths and maidens of to-day, yet on the whole it was not quite worth the candle. This was chiefly because the play was badly produced. Mr Ayliff, at work in London, had had little time to give to it, and with strict supervision withdrawn, some of the incredible old mannerisms had immediately crept back into it. The pace was allowed to get disastrously slow (a commonplace ' in Shakespeare,' but put to shame in a good modern company), speeches were spouted at the gallery and not at the person spoken to, and the clowning of the comic parts was as heartbreaking as anything demanded by the tradition. An important moral was to be drawn from this : modern clothes in themselves can do much but they cannot do it all ; only the most strenuous envisaging of the play as a modern play will work the magic. None the less, *All's Well*—admittedly less than a masterpiece—was less dull with the touch of modern atmosphere that came through than it would have been without.

The modern *Othello* was, within limits, a complete success. With the vast new impetus and life given to it by the force of the experiment, it was, though played by amateurs, the most moving performance of the play that I have ever seen. The Othello, by amateur standards, was very good. (He was dressed in a French colonial officer's uniform. It was not difficult to devise for oneself a set of circumstances in which a Moor could have taken service with a modern European power and be running a small colonial war for them. Every line in the part is true to such an idea.) One or two of the others were not good. The Desdemona herself was a novice, and the general standard of acting was what in the ordinary way would have been called ' good amateur,' and no more. But the play, when seen as a real play at last, soared beyond anything of which one had ever thought it capable. The war-talk was good, the drinking scenes were good, the jealousy of Iago towards Cassio on the score of promotion was photographic to twentieth-century life. All that one had ever believed in in the play before—and a good deal that one hadn't —fell into place with an ordered and purposeful significance. But again, as in the *Hamlet,* the justification of the experiment was that the great moments themselves not only lost nothing by the treatment but took on an unimaginably heightened beauty and pity. The Desdemona of the ordinary production is too often but a nonentity, an abstraction of the ' Shakespearean heroine '—an actress in a white robe. Make her but clear to us not as an actress but as a girl—

[75]

jog her out of the classic tradition with a fluffy white opera-cloak such as any modern girl might wear—then set the great lines of rhetoric and of passion floating around her . . . and the drama, even though played by amateurs, will gain an intensity of which the average audience has never dreamed.

From the three plays that I have seen, I conclude that there will be no other way of doing Shakespeare in the future. One, the greatest of the great, came out as pure masterpiece. Another, a bad play, had at least a glimmer of life put into it. A third, another in the line of great ones, was played by a small company of amateurs and yet was more emotional in its effect than any performance of the play for many years in London.

Where should it stop ? In this modern view of Shakespeare there is not a play, among all the great ones, that would not be the better for it. Please note that " among the great ones " is said advisedly, for the criticism of the plays implied by

[76]

doing them in a modern setting is so searching that only the best of them will survive it.

The great plays of the world deal with very elemental things. Their plot is almost always insignificant. Their theme —the transcending idea—can usually be expressed in a space of two or three words. Is *Macbeth*, when all is said and done, more than a play of ambition against conscience? Is *Romeo and Juliet* a drama of young love? Is *Antony and Cleopatra* a drama of mature passion? And is—to leave Shakespeare out of it for the minute—*The Misanthrope* a drama of a finer temperament worn out by a lower, and *The Trojan Women* a lament over the waste of war? Have ambition and conscience, love and passion, the devastation of war, and the conflict of opposing temperaments no place in the modern world? Have they not—these elementals—precisely and exactly the same place that they always had? And are not the same sun and the same stars above us all?

ICONOCLASTES

The same sun and the same stars are above us as were above Antony. And for this reason I would have the great truth—the truth to minute and immediate personal experience—insisted on rather than the lesser, fantastically unimportant, truth, to the detail of period costume. I would have them brought uncompromisingly within our own period. And the quickest way to do this, involving no violence to the text, is to use (I will now enlarge the catalogue) spats, monocles and white dress ties ; corduroys, hobnail boots, and cutty clay pipes ; shingled hair, lip-sticks, pin-curls, and silk stockings (or lisle thread stockings) precisely as the characters are well dressed or poorly dressed within our own immediate times as we know them.

Note.

The romances, *A Midsummer Night's Dream, The Tempest, etc.*, no less then than the rest. Prospero's magic island and the fairy " Wood near Athens " remain, of course, dream places, with the inhabitants dressed in whatever mystic fairy costume is necessary. But surely the intruders from the outside world, the politician Gonzalo babbling of his Utopias, and Snout, Bellows, and Flute, the village amateur-theatrical menagerie, get most of their effect from being stark portraits taken from contemporary life. Let the visitors be visitors from the world we know, or most of their point is lost.

CHAPTER IV

Recantation

I WILL now make a recantation on the
chief point that I have laboured to lead
up to in the previous chapters.

I have clamoured for spats and
monocles, pin-curls and silk stockings. I
now renounce spats and monocles, silk
stockings and pin-curls. Keep them or
abolish them, as you will. They are all so
unimportant that it will probably be
simpler, in the long run, to keep them.
But, kept or abolished, their lesson—
the truth for which they stood as symbol
—can never be forgotten.

I will recur again to my first chapter.
Think of any of the great works of literature that you know—any of the supreme
monuments to beauty that have arisen

during the centuries. Think of them at random—they will not suffer from being thrown haphazard together—from the morning freshness of Ronsard's " Mignonne, allons voir si la rose," to the morning freshness of the Chester Nativity Play, where English shepherds on the hillside, as English as ever were, are awakened by the star blazing over Bethlehem, and come to lay their gifts— a spoon, a wooden porridge bowl, a garment to keep him warm—at the feet of the newly-born god. Think of Phèdre, with Love " tout entière à sa proie attachée," and Antony's " Unarm, Eros," when he learns of Cleopatra's death, and Faustus with his " Fairer than the evening air clad with the beauty of a thousand stars," on his first sight of Helen. Think of Olivia swearing her love " by the roses of the spring," and of Juliet making young passion pure for ever with her invocation :

> Spread thy close curtains, love-performing
> night,

and Perdita among the flowers at the

F   [81]

sheep-shearers' feast, and Miranda with her cry of

> O wonder !
> How many goodly creatures are there here !
> How beauteous mankind is ! O brave new
>   world
> That has such people in it,

and of the boy who landed in France on a summer evening during the War, where he was to be killed a few months later, and felt as if " someone were giving a great party in my honour."

Think of any of these, and say, if you can, that any of them belongs to a particular clime or century. You cannot do it. For each reaches down to the heart of truth, and like the great works in other arts, the Moonlight sonata or the Dawn of Michelangelo, became immortal from the moment that it was born.

To think of their authors as dead people, or their words as period-pieces, is not only to lessen them and cheapen them, but to miss their meaning. The poem in which Ronsard and his lady go at evening to see how the rose has worn through the hot day is a sixteenth-century poem. But

THE FUTURE OF SHAKESPEARE

" it is impossible to contemplate it with
intelligent interest as a specimen of sixteenth-century poetry ; we might as well
try to refuse to be thrilled by the coming
of spring because the spring happens to be
a million years old."[1]   The thing has everlasting loveliness about it because, though
all that it has to say has been said many
times before and after, it has never been
said so well.

The masterpieces of poetry and of
character remain because, in the last
instance, the things that they have to
say have never been said elsewhere so
well.   We look back, over many centuries,
to find them, because the men who have
said them have been few and far between,
and because on one particular theme the
last word may have been said by a poet
in the dawn of Hellas, and on another by
a poet of the ' Great Century ' in France,
and on another by a poet of our own
Elizabethan renaissance, and on another
by a poet in modern Paris.   But it is

[1] Mr St. John Lucas in *The Oxford Book of
French Verse.*

[83]

about the same people that they have all written. All.

Had people changed, their words—the words of these great ones—would have no meaning for us. A poem or a play that dealt with people who had one sentiment that we did not share, or who lacked any one of the emotions that we have, would be unintelligible to us—as far beyond the hope of moving us as the loves of the triangles, or the paper snows of last year's pantomime. But they have not changed. Nothing has changed. Neither life nor death nor aspiration—nor, as Theocritus points out in his dialogue between the two Syracusan women, the unappeasable desire of husbands for their dinner.

Anatole France has a story—that he stole from someone else, who in turn stole it from someone else—of an ancient King in the East who wanted compiled for him an entire history of the human race. It was duly made for him, in a thousand volumes, and it took twenty years. When it was completed the King had no time to read it, and it was abridged (in the course of many more years) to fifty volumes. He still had no time to read it, and on his deathbed, still clamouring for his history, a further condensation, in a single huge volume, was brought to him. The King turned away from it. " Tell me in words," he said, " as my time is very short, my history of the human race." " Sire," said his chief steward, bending towards him, " I will tell you in three words the history of the human race. They were born, they suffered, and they died."

Of life only is there no end. The choicest moments of life, in their highest and most universal form, have been caught and distilled through the brain of certain rare spirits and left for us, not as a record of the past, but to fill the present with significance and splendour. How fantastic, in the face of this vast universality of experience, to pretend that the minute of time that separates us from one great genius is enough to make him aloof, remote from us, a recorder to the dead !

I have suggested that playing his plays as though they were in very fact about our twentieth-century contemporaries is on the whole the simplest and truest way of doing them. But any method that keeps this spirit is legitimate. Once train up a group of actors strong enough to realize that ruffs and doublets have no more lien on the play's meaning than have white collars and black coats—and ruffs and doublets, white collars and black coats become alike of equally little importance. Truth to the living spirit is all.

.The only way that is definitely wrong is to treat them as they are mostly treated at the moment—to invent a special set of symbols, mannerisms, movements, pronunciations, gestures, that are alone imagined to be ' Shakespearean,' and that are alone thought capable of interpreting him to our eyes. There is *nothing* that is ' Shakespearean ' ; and nothing that can be more than human. The plaster idol with his hand to his domed forehead must be torn down, and the Man—who was so human and amusing himself—is resurrected in his place.

TWO NOTES

The Speaking of Shakesperean Verse

The Old Vic

WHILE on the subject, it may not be out of place to add a word on the reasonable speaking of Shakespearean verse.

The matter is elementary, but nine actors out of ten, and ninety-nine out of a hundred members of any audience, have never heard of it.

The reasonable speaking of Shakespearean verse depends upon considerations of when in Shakespeare's life the play was written—his early period, middle period, or his late period. A use for history at last !

In the plays of Shakespeare's youth, his early period—a reference to any biography will tell one exactly which these were—Shakespeare was writing " strict blank verse." That is to say, his lines were of regular length, the full-stop or the pause in the sense came at the end of the line, the metre was perfectly even and unfaltering. The model was, of course, this:

$$\breve{} - \mid \breve{} - \mid \breve{} - \mid \breve{} - \mid \breve{} -$$

When tongues | speak sweet | ly, then | they
name | her name,
And Rosaline they call her : ask for her ;
And to her white hand see thou do commend
This seal'd-up counsel . . .

and so on. It is taken from *Love's Labour's Lost*. Line after line, for pages at a time, falls with an absolute regularity —a regularity that, unless the speaker is very careful, can easily be made to degenerate into the monotony of a jingle.

In the middle period of his life, in *Twelfth Night* and the plays of that time, Shakespeare was beginning to break up the metre with slight variants :

If music be the food of love, play on,
Give me excess of it ; that surfeiting,
The appetite may sicken, and so die.
That strain again ;—

This is different. It is a development. Notice that in two out of the four lines given, the main pause comes in the centre of the line, after " excess of it " and " that strain again." Shakespeare was making experiments, and was finding that the effect of jingle could be avoided by occasionally running the sense of one line over into the next, so that a double rhythm was kept going : one, where the end of the five-foot line demanded a close, and the second where the sense of the line carried over and arrived at a pause somewhere in the middle of the next :

                           ; that surfeiting,
The appetite may sicken.

The verse of the *Twelfth Night* period is the easiest of all to speak. Of its own accord it holds the balance perfectly between sound and sense : speak it according to its metre and you still get sense ; speak it according to its meaning and you still keep the beat. An actor has to be a very bad actor indeed not to hit off the *Twelfth Night* poetry fairly correctly.

And then comes the final phase, *The Tempest, Hamlet, Macbeth, Cleopatra.*

ICONOCLASTES

Cleopatra's rapturous greeting to Antony after battle :

> Lord of lords !
> Of infinite virtue, comest thou smiling from
> The world's great snare uncaught ?

Cleopatra's last great closing song :

> Give me my robes, put on my crown ; I have
> Immortal longings in me : Now no more
> The juice of Egypt's grape shall moist this lip:
> Yare, yare, good Iras ; quick.   Methinks I
>   hear
> Antony call ; I see him rouse himself
> To praise my noble act ; I hear him mock
> The luck of Caesar, which the gods give men
> To excuse their after wrath.

You will observe that it is now only by accident that the full-stop comes at the end of the line ; that the whole plan of the verses is to make the sense carry over to the next line ; that nearly every line ends in " I have . . .," " comest thou smiling from . . .," " now no more . . ." all phrases which demand a continuation, and receive their close *outside* the limits of the metre.

I do not by any means intend to suggest that Shakespeare was partially mad by the time that he was writing these lines, or that in the last great scenes of his greatest tragedies he was deliberately playing the fool with his medium. He had merely by that time burst and shattered the mould of " strict blank verse," and had evolved a subtler, more scattered, more wide-embracing rhythm than had ever been evolved before.

The moral for the actor is obvious. The method of speaking the middle-period verse is easy to come by : it speaks itself, sound and sense going hand in hand in perfect and effortless harmony. In the early-period verse, the whole effort must be made to avoid the jingle—to break it up wherever the opportunity presents itself. But in the later-period verse a quite contrary effort must be made—it is already so broken up that the conscious effort must be made to *hold it together*. To speak it as prose pure and simple is to shirk the issue. It is to lose some of the most complicated and grandest music ever written.

The actor speaking the early verse must be able to see that each verse is written ' for the line '—and must go out of his way to counteract it into speech that shall not sound like the clatter of a kettle-drum. In the middle-period verse he must be able to see that the verse is written with an eye to the line-and-a-half or group of lines, *i.e.*, as he would naturally speak it, and costing him no effort. And in the last plays he must be able to see that Shakespeare was working for the rhythm of the whole page, leaving entirely to chance the effect of any one individual line as it occurs :—

Of infinite virtue, comest thou smiling from.

It is the actor's business to be that ' chance.' Where the verse is loosest, he must make his correct half-comma pause at the end of every line. Where the sense apparently goes flat against beat, he must keep both the sense and the beat. If he does this well, the steady underlying rhythm that he thus keeps will be remembered by the ear at the same time that the over-tones being played above it are ravishing our souls. And the Bard's choicest effects in versification will not be entirely wasted.

THE FUTURE OF SHAKESPEARE

The Old Vic.

It may be wondered how even a short book about Shakespeare has got itself written without the big London emporium of Shakespeare, The Old Vic., yet being mentioned.

The Old Vic. has not figured in the argument largely because, up to now, it has been too busy to do Shakespeare either the old way or the new way. It just 'did' him. In the days of Mr Robert Atkins a new play was usually given every Monday night. The longest run was a fortnight. This meant the theatre being in a perpetual state of delirious rehearsal. Mr Atkins being a very fine producer, and having a solidly good company that included the genius of Mr Ernest Milton, pushed through the plays with credit, and often with very notable effect. But there was no time either for 'modern' ideas of production or for elaborate insistence on the old traditional technique. The plays were played through line for line, at speed, for

what they were worth. And this simplici-
ty and directness itself often made
them far finer representations than the
occasional West-end productions.

About the time that Mr Atkins left
the Old Vic. runs of plays were extended
to three weeks, and two stars were
engaged, Miss Edith Evans and Mr Baliol
Holloway. The increased leisure had not
happy results. Miss Evans and Mr
Holloway pulled the plays through ; but
the mannerisms and slackness of most of
the rest of the company became, to anyone
who had seen Sir Barry Jackson's *Hamlet*
—almost unendurable.

The Old Vic. is now an established institution. It has had large gifts of money.
It has had a large boom in the Press. It
has the faith of the public behind it. It
is flourishing, and increasing its scope.
But it is now precisely the time, in the
view of any unprejudiced onlooker, that
it took itself seriously in hand. The way
forward is always the way forward, and
not the way backward.

If the performances of the company as

a whole (apart from its one or two stars) are going to be as bad in the future as they have occasionally been in the past, England will then have its long-talked-of Shakespearean theatre at last—and will begin to wonder why on earth it ever wished for it.   It is an illusion to imagine that there is any honour gained or virtue acquired by having a theatre that does Shakespeare's plays because they are Shakespeare's plays. The only honour or virtue to be had out of the matter is in having a theatre that does them because it does them well.

FITZROY STREET,
   July, 1927.